Rant

E. Mackey

ISBN: 0692378979
ISBN-13: 978-0692378977

Mackey Edwin

January 24 at 6:57pm
I'm thinking, my first book may be a collection of my most
interesting statuses over the years. I'll divide the chapters by
inspirational posts, political posts, opinions, relationships, and
philosophical posts. How many of you would buy it?

CONTENTS

PREFACE

Wow! I wrote a book!
Well, I guess the first thing that I would like to express is the fact that this book was created strictly for entertainment and motivational purposes only.

With that said, please read it with an open mind, and understand that I don't profess to be an expert on anything (in this book). I don't think that I know everything, or that my opinions are any more valid than anyone else's. I am simply a person with opinions that wanted to share them.

I encourage you guys to find me on social media; I would love to interact with each of you. If/when you do find me, please know that I DO NOT debate my opinions on social media and I have zero interest in starting.

Please feel free to share anything that I have written in this book. My only request is that you credit me in your quote. If possible, please tag me. I would love to see how your friends and followers respond. I don't have a twitter account, but I can be found on Instagram (@emackeycreates) and on Facebook (Mackey Edwin). Let's connect!

Also, I wanted to keep all the posts as authentic as possible, so any typos or errors that were written in the original Facebook posts will also appear in the book.

Finally, I would like to say THANK YOU to every person that has bought, pirated, and/or shared this book. I really appreciate your interest and support!

That's all I have for now. Try not to get offended!
ENJOY!!!

-E. Mackey

1 INSPRIATON

June 16, 2013

Inspired thought is the closest thing that we have to hearing God's voice. When it's rough, push forward, when money is low, push forward, even when everyone else thinks that you're crazy, PUSH FORWARD! Your vision was given to YOU, no one else.

August 12, 2013

NEVER allow a person to tell you "focus on one thing." That's bad advice that people with limited talent give! Instead, find a way to make everything that you do work toward one goal. If you are building toward success, why on earth would you limit yourself to one way of getting there?

October 13, 2013

Always give people the opportunity to tell you no, ALWAYS TRY! Never tell yourself that an idea won't work or that someone won't help you. Just try, just ask. If they say "no," so what, who cares? It's time to stop living life so confined and restricted. I, personally, get tired of seeing talentless rich people! If they can do it, WE CAN DO IT!

May 27, 2014

2006 -2007 I was bouncing around from place to place with no place to live. One of the many people that held me down was I slept on this guy's floor MANY nights. I remember we used to count change just to try to buy the 29cent hamburgers on Sunday and Wednesday from McDonalds. I just spoke to him on the phone about current business and it hit me just how far we have come. WOW! Who knew the places we would go and things that we would achieve? People like to throw around the word "loyalty" and I don't think that they realize that at the root of loyalty is APPRECIATION! I appreciate this dude. Where I go, he's coming with me!

July 16, 2014

One if the most beautiful things in life is to come out of a struggle with someone. To have absolutely NOTHING and, somehow, turn it all around. I feel so blessed to have friends that I have shared struggle with. Lord knows, I can't wait till I'm in a position that I can bless them how they have blessed me.

November 9, 2014

Love yourself so much that people think that you are arrogant for it. It's right about that time that you won't even care what they think anyway.

November 18, 2014

My little sister was THEE meanest chick I knew. She was so full of hate and anger that I made a choice to distance myself from that energy and our relationship basically evaporated. A few months ago, she reached out to me. It was our first time (EVER) having a brother/sister talk.

Well, she rejected everything that I had to say. The conversation ended in argument, and everything went back to "normal".

A couple weeks later, she called again and this time she was open. She let go of the anger and she listened. She cried, shared some things about her that I had NO CLUE she had been dealing with, and she let it go.

In the weeks and months that passed she has become a TOTALLY different person! I never thought that I would see the day when my little sister was at peace with such a positive outlook on life.

I shared that story for 2 reasons. #1. To tell the WHOLE WORLD how PROUD I am of her growth! She is becoming such a beautiful woman!

And #2. To share with EVERY woman out there that is dealing with any form of hurt or anger that there is a light inside of you that is more beautiful than you could EVER imagine! Be brave and face your pain! Conquer your anger and make a CHIOCE that you want to be happy! There is no greater love than the love that you can have for yourself, because once you feel it, the whole world falls in line!

Your beauty will radiate and life will begin to open up for you. Make the CHOICE to be happy ladies and understand that only YOU have the power to increase or decrease your joy!

November 23, 2014

One of my major life goals is to make an impact on the world that will continue to touch people after I'm dead. Until just a few days ago, I always thought that I would have to be some huge celebrity with tons of money to do so. But, I just realized that I could actually start making an impact just by giving more love to the people around me. If I touch a life, it may inspire them to touch another life. And just like that, my life means just a little bit more.

January 12, 2015

I'm learning so much about love. (Don't put your mind in a box by thinking that I'm talking about love in a romantic sense). I'm talking about a pure, unfiltered and genuine care for other people and their well-being.

The crazy thing about love is that it not only heals the person receiving it, it also heals and strengthens the person giving it as well.

In the past few days I have had an opportunity to give love to a number of friends that were/are facing adversity and I'm learning that the expression holds so much power. Love someone! Give yourself the opportunity to be weak and watch what love does to build you up! IT IS A PRIVILEGE when a friend comes to you in pain.

Empower the people around you by allowing yourself to be weak around them. Allow them to have the privilege of showing you the love that you show to them.

January 11, 2015

I've never understood why people were so afraid to reach for happiness? For example, why fear commitment? Why on Earth would any sane person fear being loved? Or, why be afraid of following your dreams? Why fear failing when you already hate what you do?

The best aspect of life is our ability to engineer it. Why create a life filled with all the crap you DON'T want?

Happiness is a choice, not luck.

2 POLITICS

July 13, 2013

The most disgusting thing about this verdict is the fact that there are people talking about rioting! How are we ever going to better our situation if we continue to participate in the ignorance that put us there in the first place? We are ALL hurt! We are ALL disappointed!!! If you truly want a change, PLEASE STOP with the NIGGATRY! My lord, we HAVE TO find better ways of doing things! Please don't tear down everything that our ancestors have worked so hard to build and tarnish Travon's legacy by doing something stupid!

July 16, 2013

Ya know, there are things that my white friends and family simply cant understand about what it is to be black. It has nothing to do with racism or any type of intentional divide. It is just a simple fact that if you aren't black, you just wont understand what we actually experience. I am SO disappointed at some of the pro Zimmerman comments that I have seen, and I wonder, if I were killed, would they feel the same way about it? I am heartbroken that anyone could think that it is ok to kill a child... Heartbroken.

July 19, 2013

One time, a police officer pointed a gun in my face and made me spread my legs and put my hands on the hood of a car. I was in the middle of a photo shoot, and after (according to HIM) he watched us shoot for 5mins, he thought that my team had guns. I was once pulled over, while riding in the car with my uncle, because the officer wanted to know how he could afford the car that we were riding in. I was once asked to leave an establishment for asking about a $32 tab. I was accused of "not having the money to pay" so, I was trying to "get over". I politely pulled $500 out of my wallet and set it on the counter. I cant even count the number of times that I have been followed around in a store, I guess because the person wanted to be sure that I didn't steal anything? There have been MANY other situations where my race has been the SOLE cause of how I was treated, but there would be too many to mention. THIS is an example of the treatment that black people face every day! If you aren't black, you honestly wont understand how frustrating it is to constantly be harassed for no reason, then have to see Zimmerman walk free after killing someone that was walking home from a store. PLEASE stay off of my page with the excuses that are being made on behalf of George Zimmerman. He profiled Trayvon, the same way that the rest of us are profiled every day. And even if he was "defending himself", he would have never had to do so if he simply left Trayvon alone.

October 1, 2013

Ever notice that people are fighting harder to legalize marijuana than they are to get good healthcare? Priorities...

August 14, 2014

Dear white people, PLEASE stop calling us African American!!! "Black" will do just fine. We are just as American as you!

December 3, 2014

That Eric Garner thing is disgusting! ABSOLUTELY disgusting! There is no excuse, that was totally not called for.

December 7, 2014

Ya know, I don't agree with HOW a lot of black people choose to express their frustrations about race, but I DO AGREE 10,000% that their frustrations are valid!!!

I just read a post (that a white person wrote) and I was pretty disgusted with the level of ignorance that it displayed.

My personal opinion is this, if you aren't black you do not, and will not EVER, understand how REAL and complicated race relations are for us. It totally blows my mind that there is EVIDENCE of the filth that we go through and some people are STILL oblivious to what's going on.

For a non-black person to EVER open their mouth to say how "tired of hearing about race" they are is complete and TOTAL disrespect!

We are tired of LIVING it!!!

There are many blacks that dig holes for themselves. There are deadbeats, criminals and lazies in our race just like there are in EVERY other race. Those people get zero defense from me. However, there are even MORE black people (like me) that are hardworking, law abiding citizens who are SICK of being harassed and treated as 2nd rate.

There is not a single black person that I know that has not been harassed (for NO REASON) by a police officer. There is also not a single black person that I know that hasn't been followed around in a store as if they were going to steal.

Racial issues are VERY REAL in this country and to act like they aren't, or like someone is wrong for being frustrated about it, is pure disrespect.

So to all you protesters and boycotters, even though I don't agree with your methods, I DO agree that a change needs to be made and I feel that you are 100,000% right to voice yourself however you wish!!!

January 20, 2015

I honestly feel proud every time I hear Obama speak! The guy is clean cut, well spoken, charismatic, intelligent, and puts country over politics. Pure class! I honestly think that he has set the BEST example for black men that I have ever seen. FANTASTIC!

January 20, 2015

I support EQUAL rights to the FULLEST!!! That means that I HONESTLY believe that people have the right to do whatever they choose. However, the funny thing about EQUAL rights is that they include people's right to have an opinion about the dumb ish that you choose to do.

3 MY PERSONAL JOURNEY

December 29, 2012

My 2012:: Mya hosted my birthday party, worked with the Kardashians, TWERK played on Bad Girls Club, had fashion & photography published by Vogue.it, became the fashion director of a magazine, met Kanye, Chad Johnson, Usher, Diddy, Timbaland, Christina Milian, (the list goes on... I forgot all the celebs I met this year), got my own app, quit my job, built my company, did work for vitaminwater, Remy Martin, DoubleTree Hotel, Flo Rida, Chrisette Michele, A-Grade Cigars, Ace Magazine (the list goes on), helped others realize their dream(s), built relationships with millionaires, built friendships with the homeless, became a better person, met even better people. This list could go on forever, but the most important thing about my 2012 was that this was the year that it "clicked" that I can do WHATEVER I put my mind to! Life is as easy as you perceive it to be!

January 15, 2013

Just got booked for Vegas!!! Feb. 3-7th I'm there!!!

January 31, 2013

JUST got the call!!! I'm headed to Mardi Gras!!!!! TOMORROW I'm headed to Louisiana! I'll be on a FLOAT! TWERK!!!

February 2, 2013

Broadcasting LIVE from the SuperBowl MardiGras Parade!!! IM ON A FLOAT!!! TWERK!!!!

February 11, 2013

Just got the email... My song "Freaky Tonight" will be on tomorrow's episode of Bad Girls Club... DOPE!!!

February 17, 2013

SYLVESTER, I'M COMIN!!! This Saturday, I'm making Sylvester, GA... TWERK!!!

February 20, 2013

Happy 92nd birthday to my grandmother Eva Mackey!!!

August 8, 2013

I just MURDERED that Marketing exam! Thank you professor, I will accept my A now

October 4, 2013

Why do I live in Miami when I belong here?
New York...

November 19, 2013

Pretty productive day! I was asked to be a guest speaker in a college class next week, and I got casted for a small role in a big movie! Dope!

January 4, 2014

On January 4th 2006 the world lost one of its Angels on Earth. Around 4:20pm Ruth L. Brown, (My Grandmother) was killed in an auto accident. To all my friends and those that are getting to know me, she was my driving force. A lot of times she believed in me when no one else did. I love you ma.

-Glyn

January 7, 2014

It's my BIRTHDAYYYYYYYYY & my SEMINOLES brought it home!!!!!

January 14, 2014

LA, what up?

January 29, 2014

Spending the day with Jordin Sparks and her team, grabbing some exclusive photos and video, and I must say that she is a SUPER cool chick!!! Not a diva bone in her body!!!

January 31, 2014

I didn't make a ton of money, BUT this month I turned 30, visited 6 cities (across the country), worked with a couple celebrities, shoot on the beach, in the desert, and in the snow, and got over 1,627,222 hits on DerniereVie.com. I'd say 2014 is off to a fantastic start!!!

February 2, 2014

I'm selling EVERYTHING I own for dirt cheap. 2 couches, my queen sized bed, entertainment center, the in dash TV and 2 12 inch subs from my car and more. Moving to NYC and can't take any of it with me.

February 3, 2014

I'm sitting here, thinking about this move to NY, and I'm excited/blessed to have the opportunity to do so. I'm going with (basically) nothing. All I will have are the tools that I use to live/make money. My computer, camera, sewing machine, studio monitors and clothes. If I don't buy an air mattress, I will be sleeping on the floor and I will build a name in NY from scratch. I have no fear (I have God) and after all the total bull crap I have overcome in life, there is NO doubt that I will conquer NY as well. If the city doesn't want to be my lady, I will make it my b**ch, but either way success has already started.

February 12, 2014

It's official!!! My last day in Miami will be Feb. 26th. I will be having a going away party on the 25th... Details coming SOON, but expect an "E. Mackey" caliber event!

February 18, 2014

I officially have 7 more days in Miami till my move to New York. With the help of some REALLY great people, I am able to bring you guys a FREE event with FREE drinks. There will also be good music with beautiful people and I will be giving out hugs & high 5s!!! Lol, come out and enjoy the night.

February 20, 2014

Today is my grandmother's 93rd birthday!!! What a blessing! I get ALL of my sarcasm and bluntness directly from this lady! Lol, HAPPY BIRTHDAY mother!!!

February 21, 2014

OHHHH SHOOT!!! I just got my first publishing check for my song TWERK!!! BOOOMMMM!!!

February 23, 2014

In 3 days I'll be a New Yorker! Man, I've accomplished A LOT in the 3 years I've been in Miami! I've done work with/for Chrisette Michele, FloRida, Kim & Kourtney Kardashian, Remy Martin, Stoli Vodka, Bartenura Moscato, Absolut Vodka, vitaminwater, popchips, H&R Block, Doubletree Hotel, Sixt Car Rentals, and a TON of other brands. I have also met/interacted with Kanye West, Mya, Rick Ross, B.o.B, Trina, Russell Simmons, Gabrielle Union, Doug E. Fresh, Jordin Sparks, Dwyane Wade, Kevin Hart, Fatman Scoop, Robin Thicke, Christina Milian, Trinidad James, Robert Townsend, and soooo many others. I have had my music played in clubs, on the radio and used on television shows, I published a magazine, done radio interviews, did 5 fashion shows, built 2 companies & started a non profit organization (Adverb Inc., Derniere Vie and Model Citizens), learned photography, been published by Vogue.it (3 times), started an internship program, drove across the country, traveled abroad, been a guest speaker at an elementary school and 2 different colleges, volunteered with children, feed the homeless, shook hands with millionaires, held conversations with the poor, opened my heart, opened my home, and saw around $70k (without a job)... There is sooooo much more, but the point is, I will walk away from this place feeling accomplished. I'm done Miami, time to see what New York has to offer!

February 26, 2014

It's official, I live in NY... oh, yep, that's snow falling. Sheesh

March 2, 2014

Little known E. Mackey fact:: I wasn't always a sophisticated city boy. I'm actually from the country! I grew up between Miami and an itty bitty town called Monticello (outside of Tallahassee). When I was in 10th grade, I was the Grand Marshal of the town's Watermelon Festival Parade. Talk about throw back!

March 12, 2014

Tonight I'll be shooting from the riser at LA's Style Fashion Week! Can't wait to share with you guys who I'm working with tonight!

May 27, 2014

2006 -2007 I was bouncing around from place to place with no place to live. One of the many people that held me down was Kasey Blaylock. I slept on this guy's floor MANY nights. I remember we used to count change just to try to buy the 29 cent hamburgers on Sunday and Wednesday from McDonalds. I just spoke to him on the phone about current business and it hit me just how far we have come. WOW! Who knew the places we would go and things that we would achieve? People like to throw around the word "loyalty" and I don't think that they realize that at the root of loyalty is APPRECIATION! I appreciate this dude. Where I go, he's coming with me!

June 2, 2014

Who me? I'm just a "first class" citizen doing international business... Lol MAJOR S/O to one of my most valuable clients @arabellemllc for making my travel to Amsterdam possible! International first class seats are NICEEEEE! Pretty dope to think that creativity got me here! Thank you!!!

June 3, 2014

Made it safely to Europe!!!!

Made it back to the US!!! What a trip!

June 17, 2014

I just hung up the phone with Chrisette Michele. I am going to be directing the video for the first single from her upcoming project! So DOPE!!! The concept is CRAZY!!! I can't wait for you guys to see it!

June 25, 2014

So, I knew that one of the projects that I was working on was going to be sent to OWN... what I didn't know was that I would be creating it for Oprah to personally approve. OPRAH! How freggin cool is that? Oprah is going to see my work! lol, Dope!

July 30, 2014

The day that I met Ebony Payne I had LESS than nothing. I was bouncing around from place to place and living out of my car. We had ONE conversation, and couldn't have known each other for longer than 20mins, before she offered me a place to stay.

Ebony took the time to get to know and nurture EVERY one of my talents. She introduced me to music, and was the reason that I ever stepped into the booth to professionally record. She introduced me to what TJs DJs was and with that, opened my mind to an entirely new level of business.

From day ONE, within the first hour of knowing me, Ebony welcomed me into her life and has treated me as no less than blood ever since! She has sheltered me, taught me, fed me, and guided me. In times where I was in need, she has sacrificed and surprised me with unsolicited monetary blessings.

As I write, I am fighting back tears (oh wait, here they come) as I think of how incredibly BEAUTIFUL of an individual she is. EVERYTHING that I am and ALL that I accomplish is a (DIRECT result of, and) testament to how much she has unselfishly given to me.

In a million years, with a thousand tongues I could never express the level of pure gratitude that I have for her friendship. How could I ever express how much I love you? You CREATED "E. Mackey" YOU did!!! Where would I be, who would I be, if you had not come into my life when you did?

If ever, (whenever) I become the person that I have the potential to become. It will undoubtedly be because of your influence!

Ebony, you are one of few people that I consider to be my BEST friend! I love you, I love you, I LOVE YOU!

THANK YOU!!!

HAPPY BIRTHDAYYYYYYYYYYYY!!! Dirty. FREAKIN. 30!!!

September 4, 2014

My little sister and me are bonding and it feels FANTASTIC!!! I've been waiting years for this!!! *Moves every other chick to the side, my #1 girl is back!!!

September 10, 2014

Just got word that I will be going to Africa to do some work with a major artist in October... Waiting on more news, I can't speak on the rest.

September 17, 2014

Today is the first day of 4 weeks on the road for me. For the next 24 consecutive days I will be traveling... Sheesh!

Atlanta > LA > Miami > Atlanta > St. Maarten > Tallahassee > South Africa

Here we go!

September 19, 2014

Just booked a gig for BET! Boooom! Love it!

September 24, 2014

YOOOOOO!!! This September has been GREAT!!! It started with me working with Hennessy, then a cruise line, then BET, then Remy Martin/Cointreau, and I just got an email about working an event in conjunction with Visa. I was scheduled to work in 5 cities and visit 2 countries andddd I woke up to a text from Chrisette Michele saying that the video that I directed for her will be released next week!

I always talk about the struggle that it took to make things happen. But, let me stop to thank the people that have put me in a position to do dope things! Without Arthur Donaldson Kamelah Muhammad or Elora Mason having my back, NONE of the above would be possible for me! I have SOOOO much love and appreciation for you guys!

September 30, 2014

If you haven't seen it yet, here is a snippet of the video that I directed for Chrisette Michele::

https://vimeo.com/101731846

October 1, 2014

Just got my ticket confirmation for my trip to Africa! You guys are 7 days away from your timeline being FLOODED with pictures! Lol

October 8, 2014

Made it to Africa!!! Sheesh, that was a long trip!!!

October 13, 2014

Just landed back in NY and I have to say, Africa was an out of this world experience! The people are beautiful and hospitable, the food is fantastic, the internet sucks completely, but all in all, it is the one place that I can HONESTLY say that I wouldn't mind living in.

4 LOVE & RELATIONSHIPS

January 23, 2013

Ignoring a person (that cares about you) is pretty much one of the most disrespectful things that you can do... I'm sure everyone can agree.

June 6, 2013

One of the best feelings in the world is to be trusted by a woman. Like, when a woman feels safe with you. Not necessarily in a romantic sense. I mean, the way my female friends interact with me because they know that I respect and value them. I love when a woman feels safe around me.

August 4, 2013

Maybe this wont mean much coming from me, but here are a list of things that women do that men actually DONT like. Since most women are predictable, let me start by saying it is NOT necessary for you to come on my post and say "I do it for me, not for a man" or "Not ALL women". I've heard it all, trust me. This is only meant as an eye opener, not as an insult to anyone that does these things. Be you, do what you like, but be aware of what guys think about it.

For the most part we don't like:
1. Wedges (dumbest shoes ever invented)
2. High waisted shorts (no matter how sexy you are, they look crazy)
3. Implants (they look good till we learn that they aren't yours)
4. Colored contacts (seriously???)
5. Excessive tattoos (the guys that are turned on by this are not the ones that you want to date)
6. Dermal piercings (pretty much only cute to women, we think its trashy)
7. Colorful hair (Its ghetto, sorry)
8. Boxy Eyebrows (the new way that you guys are doing it were its kinda faded and boxy... sooooo dumb. its actually a turnoff)
9. Saying how independent you are. (do you want a cookie?)
10. Selfies (please just stop, please! You don't have to take a picture of yourself everyday, all day! We know what you look like)
11. Constant partying (find ways of having fun during the day. Read a book, have a picnic or something. Clubbing every week is a major turnoff)
12. Poor hygiene (this shouldn't even need to be said, but trust me, a lot of you chicks are gross)
13. Photos of you smoking (unless you are doing a themed, professional photo shoot, its not sexy.)
14. Urban "Models" (STOP!!! We have been seeing you guys oiled up & bent over for close to 10 years, time to acquire an actual talent.)
15. Drama (we can live without it! And I can live without the backlash that this post may cause)

August 4, 2013

I was accused of only being attracted to "Plain Janes" because I prefer natural, God given, beauty over "beauty" that can be bought. Sometimes I wish that I could hug every woman in the world, look her in the eyes, and say "You are beautiful exactly how you are." I don't know, I'm just not a fan of enhancements.

August 12, 2013

I honestly think that a guy needs a woman before he can truly be a man. I think it takes a woman to make us complete.

August 24, 2013

One MAJOR thing that I learned from my last relationship is this. Sometimes, not being wrong doesn't mean that you are right. There is always a better way of dealing with a situation, even if the other person is at fault. Always take the high road.

November 11, 2013

I would NEVER be with a chick that referred to me as her "nigga." I'm not with that stupid "instagram love" logic. You know, the instagram pics that say stuff like "Real b*tchs hold they n*gga down." For one, what the hell type of grammar is that? Secondly, I don't aspire to have a "hood" relationship.

March 26, 2014

Stop punishing people for the F'ed up things that your exes did to you. I don't know who you ex is (and don't care) don't call who I am into question because the last dude was an idiot. Handle your baggage before you step to someone new!

May 9, 2014

Little known E. Mackey fact:: I feel alone pretty much every day. Always have. Not on some depressed type stuff, but just in case anyone thinks that it's just them that feels that way, I'm letting you know it's not just you.

June 10, 2014

I just realized that I am so much more attracted to women that don't try to be pretty. I love to see women that are confident with who they naturally are. Someone once said that I "only date Plain Janes" after I told her she wasn't my type. It's not that, I'm just not a fan of artificial (or superficial) beauty. Being sweet and sincere is so much more of a turn on than 30 inch weave or C cup implants. (To me, at least).

June 10, 2014

Since nobody else is going to say it, I will!

There are 3 major categories that men place women in.

1.   The   sister/homie/friend::
This is the chick that we will fight over at the drop of a dime! We love this girl and don't need/want anything sexual. This girl has a special (protected) place in our hearts.

2.   The   love   interest::
This is the woman that we wake up thinking about! Those "good morning" texts that women love... THESE are the chicks that are getting them! No need to wonder if we are interested because, if you are this woman to a man, he will climb a mountain or fight a fire with a water bottle just to make you happy. This woman makes being a woman look easy! She puts little to no effort into physical beauty because she is focused on more important things! She is so naturally beautiful that she can roll out of bed with a bun in her hair (in sweat pants) and men will still drool over her in the line at the grocery store. Men LOVE this woman! This is the woman that meets the family, gets the ring, and actually "wins" in the end.

3.   The   object::
Sorry, not sorry! This is truth! A lot of women are viewed as objects by men. Obviously every man is different and some are MUCH more respectful than others, but at the end if the day no matter how good of a guy a man is there are still some types of chicks that will always be objects in a man's eyes. The sad thing about the "object" is the fact that more and more women are breaking their necks to be her! This is the chick that is plastered all over social media, half naked, overly obsessed with how she looks, how great her body is, where the next party is, and/or how "independent" she is. *Side note, independence is cool, but broadcasting it is a turnoff. A real man WANTS to provide so over emphasizing your independence is like saying you don't need or want that type of affection. Anyway, this chick is ALWAYS parting, and doesn't feel attractive unless her skin or shape is showing. This is the chick that gets hundreds of likes on social media, is always disrespected at clubs, and thinks that "men are dogs" (because we actually are, to HER). This chick may actually be BEAUTIFUL! She may have her own place, pay her own bills, or even have an education, but she STILL won't

22

have any value and it's because of how she carries herself and her materialistic views on life. She is an "object" because all men want t do is have sex with her and it will remain that way till she shows that she is worth more. She is never invited anywhere for quality time. Her dates may be expensive but they always lack substance and she is unwilling to get to know any man that she feels can't do anything for her. (Even though she is "independent").

Ladies, please stop becoming objects because (on the surface) they get more attention. We only want them for sex,

Closes chapter one of the Guy Code. Consider yourself schooled!

July 22, 2014

My ex girlfriend did some really horrible things to me. Out of hurt and anger, I treated her like total crap at times. In the years since we broke up, I learned one of the most valuable lessons that I think that I have ever learned and it shaped the way that I perceive and respond to situations.

The lesson was this:

Not being "wrong" doesn't automatically make you "right".

What it basically boiled down to is this. I was 100,000,000% justified in how I felt after she did some of the things that she did. I wasn't wrong for being hurt, and I wasn't wrong for being upset. However, how I reacted to what she did was flat out WRONG.

A lot of times, we forget that EVERY interaction that we have with other people is a series of reactions. They are reacting to how we treat them and we are reacting to how they treat us.

When we get hurt or offended, we focus so much on how WE feel, that we respond with total disregard for how our actions affect the other person. Many times our reaction creates an even bigger, (worse) situation than what we started with.

At this point in life, I ALWAYS check myself FIRST (before I open my mouth). On occasion, when I do react out of emotion, I always revisit the situation in my mind to see what I contributed to the problem.

Because I was able to be ok with acknowledging when I was/am wrong, I have so much more peace and I'm better equipped to defuse situations to preserve valuable relationships.

I said all this to say to everyone, get over yourself!!! In almost every disagreement there is something that you could have done differently to arrive at a better outcome. Being petty, hateful, vengeful and/or jealous won't bring an ounce of value to your life.

Swallowing your pride for the sake of salvaging a relationship will. (By "relationship" I mean any type of relationship, not just romantic ones).

August 24, 2014

You can't love someone and hold on to pride at the same time. Some people would rather lose a great person simply because they refuse to simply say "I'm sorry" or own up to being wrong. Be an adult...

September 13, 2014

Ladies, please stop making it a man's responsibility to make you happy. Find happiness for yourself! That way, you will be in a better position to appreciate when a man SHOWS you love and you will stop falling for the people that SAY the things that you want to hear.

November 9, 2014

When I meet a woman (that I'm interested in) I immediately try to imagine her as my wife. I pay attention to how she speaks, what she is interested in, the type of people that she hangs out with, (and so on) and I try to imagine her being the mother of my children. If I can't see it, she gets ZERO attention and none of my conversation.

I'm also a "one at a time" type of dude. I will give a woman my full, undivided, attention so that I can take time to focus on what she brings to the table and how she appreciates/receives what I bring to the table with no distractions. With that said, the moment that she shows me that we aren't compatible, or that she isn't worth my time, I cut everything off.

At the end of the day, people can perceive me however they want. They can say what they want to say about me, and they are free to form whatever opinion that they choose based on facebook posts and instagram pictures but the cold hard truth is that I am ALWAYS a man.

I treat people how I want to be treated and when that isn't an option, I treat them how they treat me. I have NEVER intentionally disrespected, or mistreated anyone and when it is brought to my attention that I am wrong about something, I don't debate it. I own up to it, apologize, brush my shoulder off and move forward.

Any person that has ever talked to me for 5mins can tell you that I default to blunt honesty. Games, lies and any other form of beating around the bush is an absolute waste of my time and energy. (I'd much rather just say what I have to say and keep it moving). When I play, I show my hand and put all my cards on the table.

I'm open with how I feel (and I express it) and a woman is more than welcome to call me "soft" or accuse me of "being in my feelings"... it would only show me that she is a little girl that hasn't matured enough to appreciate the fact that adults communicate things like that.

I said all that to illustrate how I feel that dating should go. I think that we (men and women) have such f'ed up interactions with each other because people refuse to put the baggage to the side to give someone new a fair chance at getting to know us.

We make other people accountable for our emotions and get upset and loose interest when they don't have the time, patience, or interest in "fixing" us when what we should have been doing was fixing ourselves.

We put up walls out of fear of being hurt and rejected and in the process, we become the EXACT person (to the other person) that we are trying to protect ourselves from.

I said all of what I said because I want to make it cool to be honest with people. I want to make it cool to be honest with people that you aren't interested in, as well as being open with people that you are. I would love to see the day when a man can tell a woman how he feels and she not try to emasculate him because that expression makes her feel uncomfortable because she doesn't even love herself.

I'll be the first person to step to the plate. Who else want's to take accountability for their baggage and step to the next person that they date 100% correctly? Or do you guys want to continue to be damaged and play hard for social media?

I'll wait...

November 12, 2014

You know what's sexy? A woman that you can have an actual conversation with! A conversation where thoughts, ideas and opinions are expressed and expounded upon. A conversation that is free of slang and gossip. A conversation that goes deeper than current events and somehow finds itself in the depths of future ambitions. What's even more sexy is when she lusts for it. When that woman gets excited and looks forward to having that conversation with you. The cherry on top, the one thing that will REALLY get me wrapped up in her, is for her to say, "I want a man that can teach me things." Gives me freakin chills!

Your body is amazing, but I'm trying to get your mind naked. Sex me mentally.

November 18, 2014

I met somebody that I actually like... Now, all other conversation is like "whomp whomp whomp"... It's nice to feel like you are giving your attention to someone that actually deserves it.

November 19, 2014

Realizing that I have a responsibility to love the women in my life in such a way that it sets the standard for how the men that they date should love them.

I never realized how vital it is for a woman to have men in their life that they can trust and depend on.

I never really looked at it as my responsibility to "heal" a woman (and it's not). But, when it comes to the women closest to me, it IS my responsibility to be a man to them. That role encompasses being someone that they can be open with that they feel safe confiding in. I hope that I can be a better example.

December 7, 2014

I have a new outlook on relationships. I intend to gain more than what I had and give more than I get. I'm excited about the next person that I get to love.

December 26, 2014

I just want to apologize to the women that have followed me for years on here. In the past, I posted a lot of TRUTHS about (my interactions with) women. But, in the past few months I have learned that, even though it was true, what I said came from a place of bitterness, hurt and disappointment in my available dating pool.

What I am learning is that it doesn't matter that there are bad women out there. It doesn't matter that I may meet them, date them, and be taken advantage of. What matters is that I stay true to me, and I treat every woman that I meet with the exact same love and respect that I would give if I knew for certain that she is the one.

I had to learn that being afraid to love a woman, or being defensive, is an immature way of getting to know a person. A healthy, mature, way of dating is putting yourself last and being available to understand the other person's needs.

Again, I'm sorry for all that stuff that I said... I'm starting to realize that there is more going on. Mostly, that I have to check myself before I can check anyone else.

January 21, 2015

I just realized that a lot of women would rather change the men that they are attracted to, rather than change the men that they are attracted to...

As the preachers would say, "You'll get that one in the parking lot."

5 RANDOM THOUGHTS & OPINIONS

January 27, 2013

I have always been so "Go Go Go" that I never really took the time to appreciate how precious and beautiful that a woman's feelings are... When a woman cares for a man (even as friends) that is something magical!

February 2, 2013

People will call you crazy if you tell them your vision. Those same people will call you arrogant if you tell them what you have accomplished. I'm at a point in life where I realize that my life is based on my actions, not other people's opinion. Thank you father! Let them talk...

April 9, 2013

There are BILLIONAIRES among us and people get on social media flashing hundreds... You look silly!

April 11, 2013

Some people simply don't deserve 2nd (3rd, 4th, 5th, 6th...) chances. They are who they are, and that is it! Sadly, you can't choose your family, but you do have 100% control over who you allow to be in your life.

May 18, 2013

I'm sorry, but Kanye West does not get the credit that he deserves. The guy is an absolute genius! Too bad people are so ignorant to art that the only way that they can justify creativity is by throwing the word "Illuminati" at it.

May 20, 2013

I honestly believe that a man needs a woman... I really do.

May 21, 2013

Thank you father... I dont even need a reason, I just know that you are working on my behalf.

May 25, 2013

I'm realizing that being the person that I want to become means being alienated by people... Average minds won't get it, but I just feel that my life should be about more than just myself. Life is bigger than me.

June 24, 2013

It's so funny reading all these statuses about "love yourself"...lol, crazy thing is, as soon as you do, people will accuse you of being arrogant. I'm at a point in life where I'm ok with being called names. I'm ok if I can't afford something, and I'm ok if someone doesn't find me attractive. It's not so much that I "love me", I just figured out that on the list of things that REALLY matter in life, outside opinions are pretty close to the bottom.

July 14, 2013

Hatred is disgusting no matter what color your skin is...

July 26, 2013

It's just something magical about being a SEMINOLE! Dang! Florida State University Alumni and proud of it!

August 4, 2013

I have this issue where once you lie to me, I really can't vibe with you anymore. Lying to me is pretty much one of the worst things that you can do to me.

August 6, 2013

I absolutely suck when it comes to finding good women. But, when it comes to friends, I have the BEST that the world can offer! I'm always amazed at how beautiful the people around me are! God could not have blessed me to know better people. To all of you out there that actually KNOW me, that have helped me, supported me, and blessed me throughout life, I love you! Thank you!

August 11, 2013

Dear Apple, I love your products (for the most part), but you have the WORST charger cords on the planet!!! Now I can't work, & I have to buy a $80 replacement! Thanks a lot! MacBook Pro

August 18, 2013

The deeper that I get into this MBA program, the more I realize that life is so much bigger than we make it. Money is as abundant as air to some people. Why not strive to do business in those arenas? The wealthy are no smarter or talented than the rest of us, they just have a better understanding of how to use their resources.

Rant

August 27, 2013

Have you ever thanked God for no reason?

September 14, 2013

Added London to my phone so I can always know what time it is where Jasmine Chantel Norris is ☺

September 21, 2013

I just want to say I love you to everyone. Male, female, white, black and other... Even if you don't like me, I love you anyway. Let me know if I can ever help you. If I can, I will.

October 17, 2013

RELATIONSHIPS will take you 10x further, 10x FASTER than money every single day of the week! RESPECT EVERYBODY, blessings come from every corner! I may not have a ton of money, but I have superior relationships!

October 24, 2013

Thank you father for the times when I had nothing! Thank you father for EVERY struggle, for every day that I didn't have a place to live or food to eat. Thank you father for showing me TRUE struggle. And thank you for every angel that you have placed in my life. Your work will be done! Without fail.

October 25, 2013

There is nothing more perfect in this world than a woman!

November 3, 2013

I'm sorry, I can't vibe with a liar...

November 9, 2013

People are making babies like sandwiches! You guys realize that those are people that you are creating, right? Dang yo, not judging anybody (your life wont affect me one bit) but, just understand that having a child isn't something to take lightly.

December 1, 2013

Just replaced the motor in my granddad's antique sewing machine... Yup, I fix stuff too... Lol

December 23, 2013

Nobody REALLY knows about my personal situation growing up. In a nutshell, it was pretty much me bouncing around from house to house, or family to family because my father was in jail, (or prison) and my mother was with a man and she didn't want me there to "ruin her relationship." She put me out when I was 13 (17 years ago) and, as a result, I honestly HATE the holidays (all of them) and pretty much any other "family" oriented observance. I have very little experience, or faith in "love" with a woman because my experience has always been that women expect men to abandon our hurt and wounds to cater to theirs, and obviously I have my own. At any rate, my mother just called me and pretty much told me that she was young when she had me and that she had been hurt and abused so she shouldn't be held accountable for things that she did in the past. She attributes my feelings of hurt and abandonment to me "holding a grudge" and she suggests that I "get over it." My parents divorced when I was 4, so I don't know much about their marriage, but my mother just told me that December 23, 1977 was "the worst day of her life." That was the day that she married my dad. Imagine how I felt to indirectly be told that my existence was a part of one of the worst days of my mother's life. Kinda crazy how life goes. I am starting to understand that people (no matter who they are) have very deep scars and it makes me want to be alone, in a box, forever. I said all that to say this, to all the women out there. Pain, hurt, and abandonment IS NOT exclusive to YOU. Men are people and we have issues that we have to deal with as well. Expecting a man to come into your life and solve your problems is unfair and extremely selfish. Expecting a man to "accept" the fact that "you have been hurt" and to "prove himself" without you taking the time to do the same for him is selfish as well. It is no person's job to fix you. It is our responsibility to look at our own situations and fix ourselves. It is not fair for a child to be mistreated because of the actions of his father. It is not fair for a man to be mistreated because of the actions of your father. And it is not fair to drag the next person into your personal issues or mess. As you can see, we all have our own. Just had to get some stuff off my chest. Please DO NOT give me any pity posts. I don't need any motivational words. I'm fine. I'm just sharing a thought.

January 24, 2014

Ladies, you are BEAUTIFUL!

February 3, 2014

Little known E. Mackey fact:: I started college as a pitcher for Albany State University. I broke my jaw after transferring and never played baseball again.

February 5, 2014

I'm so sick of people with subpar ambition and low self esteem calling me arrogant. It gets old. Don't be mad at me that you don't value yourself. That's YOUR problem.

February 20, 2014

WhatsApp was sold to Facebook for $19 BILLION today. Crazy part, the owner crated whatsapp after facebook wouldnt hire him! lol Talk about creating your own destiny! lol DOPE

February 28, 2014

There is a difference between genuinely wanting to share your happiness with others and being boastful. I honestly think that a lot of people try to get validation from facebook. Proclaiming how great your life is to "stunt on haters" is disgusting! Everyone has good days, everyone has bad days and everyone struggles, there is no shame in that. Struggle is temporary but an f'ed up personality is something that you have to live with!

March 6, 2014

I don't know... Short women just do it for me. 5'5 and under... I love em!

March 11, 2014 a repost of Eva Liz

The less you associate with some people, the more your life will improve. Any time you tolerate mediocrity in others, it increases your mediocrity. An important attribute in successful people is their impatience with negative thinking and negative acting people. As you grow, your associates will change. Some of your friends will not want you to go on. They will want you to stay where they are. Friends that don't help you climb will want you to crawl. Your friends will stretch your vision or choke your dream. Those that don't increase you will eventually decrease you.

–   The Power of Association

May 9, 2014

Little known E. Mackey fact:: I feel alone pretty much every day. Always have. Not on some depressed type stuff, but just in case anyone thinks that it's just them that feels that way, I'm letting you know it's not just you.

July 13, 2014

FYI:: To the ladies that advocate doing squats and all these exercises for your butt. Just so you know, a hard booty is NOT sexy! Sorry, we (men) can appreciate your effort, and we love a toned woman, but when you stop being soft it's kind of a turnoff. Nothing wrong with getting in shape and being healthy, but it's also nothing wrong with loving your natural body.

July 29, 2014

There is SO MUCH good music out there. If you only listen to the radio you'll never hear it!

August 11, 2014

I actually spend hours a day trying to figure out how I can put other people on. I actually fantasize about things that I can do to help other people do what they do. I can't wait till I'm in a position to just make a call and drastically change people's lives.

August 16, 2014

There is a 13 year-old, black, girl pitcher in the Little League World Series that has a 70 mile per hour fastball. EVERYTHING about that sentence blows my mind! Mo'Ne Davis, I GOTTA find out when she's pitching so I can watch.

November 25, 2014

We all know the story that says that Harriet Tubman could have freed more slaves if they knew they were slaves. I wonder how many she helped escape that never realized that they were free?

I agree 100% that there is mental slavery in 2014. The crazy thing is, black people have become their own slave masters!

December 27, 2014

Social media has given us way too much access to other people's negative energy and ignorance.

January 4, 2015

It has been 9 years to the day that my grandmother passed away. I wish that she could have seen some of the things that I have accomplished and some of the places that I have been in life. She always told me that I was going to "be somebody" one day. I'm almost there. I love you momma!

March 1, 2013

I'm so sick of hearing everyday people say "Started From The Bottom!" Like seriously, did you walk up stairs or something?

June 2, 2013

You chicks don't ever get tired of ALWAYS partying or taking pictures in bathrooms? Sheesh! It's old!

June 27, 2013

I deleted a BUNCH of people today! Please keep your opinions on your own page. I don't post to hear what you have to say.

October 28, 2013

Dear Negros, it is ok to give someone else credit! Contrary to popular belief, you won't die! It also wont make you any less talented or less of a person. Believe it or not, it actually feels good to give someone else credit! I encourage you all to try!

6 YA FEEL ME?

January 27, 2014

Dear black people, Daft Punk is a LEGENDARY duo!!! They have been around for about 15 years (or more) and they were already one of the biggest names in electronic music WAYYYYYY before "Get Lucky". The helmets aren't new either, it's kinda their thing. I just wanted to give you guys a quick history lesson just in case you guys thought that they were one of the new aged, bubble gum artists that keep popping up.

October 31, 2014

If you are from Florida (ESPECIALLY Miami) the most EPIC moment in the club is when the DJ plays Trick Daddy and that part "HOL' UP, WAIT ONE MUTHA F*CKIN MIN." Comes on! Lol, it gets no more live than that! MIAMI stand up!!! Lol

November 16, 2014

If you were born in 199anything, I feel like you aren't old enough to have an opinion about Aaliyah or the movie. When they make a Young Thug movie, then the 90s babies can have an opinion.

December 5, 2014

Dear white friends and family, let the record show that black people DO NOT want to be called African American. You have my word, it's ok to call us "black"! Please note that "Nigger" (and all variations) is OFF LIMITS indefinitely. Lol

January 3, 2015

JUST DELETED my 1st person of 2015 for posting a fight video. Anymore volunteers?

7 RANTS

January 17, 2013

In case you guys didn't' know, there are actually people that are good at more than one thing. "Focus on one thing" is bad advice that is given by people with limited talent...

January 27, 2013

Let me clarify something. I don't have a problem with WOMEN, I LOVE women! You know, hard working, dependable, loving, caring people that have respect for themselves. Not all females are WOMEN, don't get it twisted! With that said, if it offends you when I call out WACK females, feel free to unfriend, or make changes in your life! I refuse to put a chick on a pedestal simply because she is female. My pedestal is reserved for REAL WOMEN

May 29, 2013

In Miami, people spend WAY too much time trying to look good and no time trying to BE good! Keep the clubs, keep the bottles, and keep the rental cars. I'll keep pushing till the plan works.

I would like to confess something. I really hate Miami! The people here are too shallow and talk entirely too much! The value system (ha, "value system") is crap, and people are overly focused on manufactured "beauty" and a pretend lifestyle. This place is not where it's at.

May 30, 2013

I hate how people use The Bible when it is convenient... Be consistent.

June 7, 2013

Until you hold yourself to a standard, don't set expectations for other people! I am noticing that that is a huge problem with (black) people. We expect everyone else to bring this or that "to the table", but we rarely stop to look at what we contribute. Hold YOURSELF to a standard.

June 23, 2013

I guess I'm missing this skin tone documentary... Sad that we even need one. After all that black people have been through (because of skin color) leave it to BLACK PEOPLE to continue the ignorance by making one complexion "better" than another. I swear, as a whole, we are backwards and lost!

July 3, 2013

It frustrates men when it seems that a woman would rather "fix" a weak man than trust a good one. Too many times have I met beautiful woman that were stuck on worthless dudes, only to tell me that "I'm perfect, but they aren't ready." The fact is, a lot of women actually do know what they want. It's just that they are so full of fear that they are paralyzed when they get it. Ladies, don't 2nd guess a good man, you are WORTH having him! (Some of you at least). *Please no debates, I will delete you.

July 5, 2013

I think that I have just read the most DISGUSTING status of all time! If all you have to offer is a pretty face and name brands, you are pretty much worthless. I am so tired of these "South Beach" mentalities.

July 13, 2013

I have 5,000+ friends, 800+ subscribers and 400+ pending requests. Not to mention, 700+ more people on my fan page. If you dont like what I post, just delete me. I wont even notice you're gone!

February 5, 2014

I'm so sick of people with subpar ambition and low self esteem calling me arrogant. It gets old. Don't be mad at me that you don't value yourself. That's YOUR problem.

February 9, 2014

I'm sorry, you have to actually be an intelligent, thought processing (open minded) individual to be my friend. We don't have to agree on everything, but if we don't, you need to have a solid reason for why you feel the way that you do that is based on YOUR research and convictions. Birds of a feather flock together so I can only keep company with leaders. The people lacking ambition, self esteem and/or motivation can't even get conversation from me, and if you consider what you do as "on the side" we surely don't have anything to talk about. Get some fire inside of you! Stand for something! Have something that you are willing to fight for, have something that you are willing to sacrifice for. Have passion or have a freakin seat.

February 28, 2014

There is a difference between genuinely wanting to share your happiness with others and being boastful. I honestly think that a lot of people try to get validation from facebook. Proclaiming how great your life is to "stunt on haters" is disgusting! Everyone has good days, everyone has bad days and everyone struggles, there is no shame in that. Struggle is temporary but an f'ed up personality is something that you have to live with!

March 26, 2014

Stop punishing people for the F'ed up things that your exes did to you. I don't know who you ex is (and don't care) don't call who I am into question because the last dude was an idiot. Handle your baggage before you step to someone new!

June 5, 2014

I'm realizing that I'm the guy that women just like to look at. They are too afraid to be with someone like me. You can't look too good, be too nice, be too talented, be too honest, or travel too much because women don't like that. If you are "too good" a woman won't want you because they think that every other woman wants you. Since "every other woman" wants you, somehow that makes you a "dog".

It seems to me that the more time a man spends making himself better, the less "real" he becomes and thus the less appealing.

The less time a man spends bettering himself the more the woman can "fix" him and the more appealing he becomes because a woman can imagine how "good" he "can" be "when" she "fixes" him.

I used to get so upset because I was going out of my way to be perfect and I was always getting rejected. But now I understand that I was never the problem, it was them!

I can't and WON'T fix a broken & insecure woman. That is not my job.

I will show you who I am and from there you can take it or leave it, but chase you I will not.

My philosophy is this, (male or female) a person should think so highly of you that they can't even see anyone else. If you have to convince a person to love you, they are not the one.

With all that said, I leave you guys with this. Other people's fear and insecurities are their own problem to deal with. If a person is afraid of (or can't see) how "good" you are, leave them where they are. Don't bother trying to prove anything to them. Someone out there is wishing they could take their place.

July 6, 2014

I've never been motivated by money. I actually think it's pretty disgusting when people say things like "Money over everything." You have to live an F'ed up, uncultured existence to think like that! VALUE over everything! Happiness is a priority and to me, money is at the bottom of the list of things I value in life.

July 31, 2014

Just found out from someone close to me that other people "close to me" have (and have always been) bashing me behind my back. I was told that they were critical of my life decisions and had nothing but negative to say about me. My response? HYSTERICAL LAUGHTER!!! Seriously! I'm so busy living my life that I couldn't give 2 craps about what anyone else has going on. It amazes me that people actually entertain themselves by talking about others behind their backs. I get a kick out of saying it to your face... Lol

August 15, 2014

I was just just called "uppity" and said to "have a silver spoon in my mouth" by someone because I want black people to take accountability for their actions. HILARIOUS!

I make it a point to be VERY transparent about my past. It is no secret that a STRUGGLED to have what I have. I have ALWAYS been poor. When I was 4 years old, I was dropped off to live with my grandmother in the projects (where I grew up) to add to it, the project building that we lived in burned down. So, not only did we have nothing, we lost the little that we had in the fire.

I grew up practically without my mother or father. I bounced around from place to place, up until I graduated from high school.

I put MYSELF through college. It took me 8 years to get my bachelors degree, because while I was in school, I was homeless twice and lived out of my car. I payed for one class at a time, and even had a semester where I could only afford to take one class and I went to it on my LUNCH BREAK. I was working a construction type job, so I went to that class dirty every day.

To think of the ABSOLUTE struggle that I had to endure to get to where I am, and have some person that doesn't have a clue who I am, say that I have a silver spoon in my mouth is one of the most offensive things that I have ever heard! I fought, clawed, cried and BLEED to be where I am.

If it makes me "uppity" to come from the projects, a parentless home and homelessness, to EARN an education and build a company and life where I get to travel and meet interesting people then so be it!

I F*CKING KNOW STRUGGLE! I have had a police officer point a gun in my face when I was just minding my business at a photo shoot, so I also KNOW HATRED, RACISM and PROFILING first hand!

I could not care less if any one of you agree with anything that I have to say. But you WILL NOT attack my character!

I believe what I believe because I KNOW the power that lies in every single one of us! I know the absolute potential that each individual has to change their lives. So, I WILL NOT EVER be a person that will blame "the white man" society, media or any other external factor for why we are not advancing as a race. I F*CKING BLAME US!

Me saying that black people need to help themselves is NOT me being uppity, it is me speaking as a person that has had LESS than nothing and recognizing that if I can change my life, then everyone else can too!

Black people are NOT oppressed and we are not victims! We are lazy, entitled, unwilling to take responsibility for our own actions and we get offended the moment someone calls us out on our bull sh*t!

We are so full of hate that you get mad a another black person for being successful? We are sellouts and "Uncle Toms" for

---

bettering our lives? I'm accused of not understanding the struggles that black people face because I have degrees? This is how we treat each other and we have the nerve to blame someone else for our F'ed up situation? Kick rocks yo!

October 10, 2014

Just read a status that REALLY upset me! It seems that this young lady feels that Hispanics don't need to learn English in America because Americans need to learn Spanish. THAT arrogant and disrespectful mentality is the type of stuff that REALLY pisses people off!

First of all, when you go to another country it is YOUR responsibility to learn how to maneuver. You don't come, (ESPECIALLY when you come to use our resources) and expect the natives to cater to you!

Secondly, in case you didn't know, English is the international language (not Spanish). So if there were any language that any person on the planet "needs to learn" it would be English.

Lord knows I don't have any issue with any group of people, but I do have an issue with people that come to MY country with that arrogant attitude like we owe them something.

November 12, 2014

In case any of you are waiting on my opinion of the Kim K. Paper Magazine cover, it is this. YES, I actually am a fan of Kim's. (If you remember, I worked on her show a couple years back, I think that she is a super cool chick). HOWEVER, I thought that the cover was trash. Sorry, not something that a married woman or a mother should do. Now, before you guys get upset (like I actually give a crap) let me just say that I am all for a woman's right to do whatever she wants. But, I think that having the right to do something doesn't give you a free pass to behave like you don't have class.

You can have the fattest butt and perkiest boobs on the planet, but (as a woman) your sexiest attribute will always be your class.

(I didn't ask to hear anybody else's opinion, let me just make that clear).

November 13, 2014

I had somebody that I really respect get mad at me yesterday and say "I'm about to end this (business) relationship... I laughed and thought, "who gives a flying ****?"

Let me tell you guys something, at the end of the day, NOBODY makes or breaks you but YOU. Nobody gave me any handouts, I EARNED everything that I have, so I will ALWAYS be good!

Get to a point where you can approach any situation with that same confidence and you can walk away from any situation the same way!

November 15, 2014

106 & Park is canceled!!! I count that as a WIN for black youth! Now we need to get love & hip-hop on the chopping block.

November 20, 2014

Listen, someone ran into our (FSU) library and opened fire. I studied there MANY nights into the am hours of the morning. I happen to know that MANY students from FAMU and TCC utilize Strozier as well, so when I say OUR, I actually mean OUR!

I just read the most disgusting post on IG from somebody that I actually had a lot of respect for. In it, she tried to say that if the shooting were at FAMU, FSU would be fighting to get the school shut down.

As a BLACK FSU alumni, and a former student of an HBCU I think that I am more than qualified to say that I am SICK of all of you militant @$$ black people that insist on turning EVERY situation into a plot against black people by "the white man".

Nobody at FSU hates FAMU. Black people that go to FSU don't think that we are "better" than anyone at FAM. I am so sick of all the hate and ignorance that I don't know what to do!

Nobody is plotting on us! There is no conspiracy! There are productive black people and black people that give the race a bad name. The same is true for other races.

We do all this fighting because we are tired of being blamed and stereotyped for the actions of a small segment of the black community but turn around and blame ALL white people for the ignorance of a small segment of people from their race.

Your ignorance won't allow you to see that YOU are the EXACT person that you are fighting against!

At the end of the day, this was a school shooting! How the F' did this turn into a racial issue?

January 2, 2015

It takes a special type of hate for fans of teams that have long been home on the couch to come out the woodworks and comment about FSU. FSU has WON 29 games in a row, were defending National Champions, and competed toward a National Championship this year. Were we not supposed to be proud of that? Where we wrong for celebrating the team's accomplishments? Lastly, had the shoe been on the other foot and it was YOUR team that did all that (ha, right) wouldn't YOU be as happy and proud as we were?

Don't be butt holes. FSU has NOTHING to be ashamed of!

So, haters from FAMU, your team doesn't even exist. Haters from UF, yours doesn't either. And UM fans, I think that FSU CURRENTLY holds the ACC Championship. Soooo? lol

1 loss since 2012. Nole Blooded!

January 17, 2015

Amber Rose gets ZERO praise from me, and if YOU praised her, I better not hear anything from you about bettering the black community... PERIOD!

Never mind having basic self respect, y'all do understand that this chick is a mother, right? I thank God that I will NEVER be able to see my mother half naked, plastered over the internet with her entire body covered in tattoos.

What happened to standards? What happened to taking pride in being a lady? I am ashamed and disgusted with this raggedy generation! We glorify stupidity and trash then get upset when our culture and way of life isn't valued by other races. Kick rocks to ANYONE that objects!!!

PS. I don't give a crap WHO you are, if you come on my status disagreeing or debating, I'm deleting you. The garbage WILL NOT be coming into 2015 with me.

January 19 at 1:58am

Camera: $3,000 || Lens: $2,000 || Camera bag: $100 || Reflector: $45 || MacBook Pro: $1,500 || Adobe Photoshop: $500 || Final Cut Pro: $500

Please consider that the next time you want to book a shoot with a professional.

8 RELIGION

Thinking of what my life situation was on Monday and looking at what it is NOW and thanking God for how UNBELIEVABLY fast I was delivered from that messed up situation!!! Struggle is temporary, FAITH is everlasting and God is REAL! PERIOD! Thank you father!!!

October 5, 2013

I have come to realize that when things seem out of place and when they feel like they have fallen apart, it is God shifting you into a better situation... Life has a way of nudging you on the right path. It's pretty dope if you let it happen. Give God room to work.

February 11, 2014

Thank you father for the heartache from my ex. Thank you father for not being able to find a job after I graduated. Thank you father for every rejection from women that I thought that I was interested in, and for every broke day, hard day, and struggle. I thought about what my life would be like if I never went through any of the pressure and pain and I realized that it would NOT have been the life for me! Thank you father for blessing me with pain, I see what you are doing up there!

September 27, 2014

Never underestimate God's ability to place the EXACT right people in your life at the EXACT right time. On the same note, don't neglect the fact that he will also REMOVE the people that are toxic to you. In all that you do, in every situation, it is important to remain positive. Positivity creates space for God to work.

December 25, 2014

Am I the only person that gets SUPER offended when people write "xmas" as opposed to "Christmas"? I just don't understand how people could just remove Christ from his day?

December 25, 2014

Since it's Christmas, I thought I'd remind everyone that Jesus is a Capricorn. So, I guess I don't have to mention what the best zodiac sign is…

9 QUOTE ME

March 12, 2013

Find a man with vision and be patient through the struggle. The value lies in his mind, not his pockets.

April 6, 2013

People are so broken... I never really realized how poorly people perceive life. The worst prison is a negative perception.

April 14, 2013

Speak up! Keep it real with people... People can call you mean or rude but, nobody can ever call you fake!

June 27, 2013

It's always better to tell people what the NEED to hear. Sugarcoating doesn't help anyone. Being honest helps people grow.

September 17, 2013

The prize never goes to the person that is the best, it goes to the person that gave the most effort!

January 10, 2014

Thank you father for blessing me enough to know that I don't need a reason to say "Thank you father."

January 10, 2014
Every struggle is a blessing.

January 11, 2014

When you look at life in terms of value, not money, it takes much less to make you happy. When you are happy, it takes much less to gain more.

February 25, 2014

"Broke is temporary but poor is eternal."

March 1, 2014

You might be looking for all the right things but rejecting it because it's not packaged how you want it. Take time to open the wrapper.

April 16, 2014

Deadbeat mothers exist, trust me I know.

April 17, 2014

The crazy thing about wanting to be rich is the fact that you can't be afraid to go broke!

June 23, 2014

Success isn't buying a $400 bottle in a club. Success is SELLING a $400 bottle in a club.

June 26, 2014

There is something about faith that just makes things fall perfectly into place!

June 29, 2014

Nothing worse than a person that can't acknowledge when they are wrong and simply apologize for it.

July 27, 2014

You can't expect a person that never struggled to understand sacrifice.

July 30, 2014

There is no faster way to reach your goals than by helping the next person reach theirs.

November 9, 2014

Love yourself so much that people think that you are arrogant for it. It's right about that time that you won't even care what they think anyway.

November 30, 2014

The slightest amount of doubt is enough to ruin an entire prayer.

January 21, 2015

Some women are so busy looking for Superman that they never notice Clark Kent.

January 25, 2015

Don't be mad when you get what you prayed for. (Giving myself advice… and taking it!)

ABOUT THE AUTHOR

E. Mackey is a director, photographer, and entrepreneur that is best known throughout his social media for his creativity and BRUTIAL, unapologetic HONESTY.

He currently travels the world doing various creative projects as well as working to build infrastructure in developing countries.

To learn more about E. Mackey, or to follow his journey, connect with him on Instagram: @emackeycreates.

ABOUT THE AUTHOR